The Scholastic FunFact Book of

MONSTERS

SCHOLASTIC BOOK SERVICES

NEW YORK · TORONTO · LONDON · AUCKLAND · SYDNEY · TOKYO

Written by:
Carey Miller

Art and editorial direction:
David Jefferis

Text editing and additional research:
Sue Jacquemier, Ingrid Selberg

Design assistant:
Iain Ashman

Picture research:
Caroline Lucas

Natural history consultant:
Dr L. B. Halstead, PhD DSc

Illustrators:
John Francis, Malcolm McGregor,
Michael Roffe, Christine
Howes, Mike Baber

Additional photography:
David Jefferis, Peter Mackertich

Acknowledgements:
We wish to thank the following individuals and organizations
for their assistance and for making available information and
photographs from their collections: Associated Newspapers
Ltd, Columbia Warner Distributors Ltd, Gerry Anderson
Productions Ltd, Federico Arboro Mella, Keith Wilson, Radio
Times Hulton Picture Library, Royal Geographical Society.

12 11 10 9 8 7 6 5 4 3 2 1   6   8 9/7 0 1 2 3/8
Printed in the U. S. A.   02

**Scholastic Book Services
An Usborne Book
One of the Scholastic FunFact Series**

About this book

People have always been fascinated by
monsters, and many stories about them have
been told through the ages. Some monsters,
such as dragons, come from ancient myths and
legends. Dinosaurs and other prehistoric animals
can also be called monsters. Even today there is
some evidence to suggest that strange, unknown
creatures may exist in areas of the world that
people have not fully explored.

Strange beasts have been reported lurking in
mountains, forests, lakes and oceans. Are the
accounts of them to be believed?

This book contains eye-witness reports,
stories and detailed information about all kinds
of monsters: some are imaginary, some are real,
and some are unsolved mysteries.

The Scholastic FunFact Book of

MONSTERS

Contents

The word "monster" is used to describe any strange creature. It comes from the Latin word *monstrum* (an omen). At one time people thought that the appearance of an abnormal creature was an omen, or warning, of an unusual event. The word is most often used, however, of things that are particularly big, fierce, or frightening.

There have been monsters of various kinds throughout history. Some actually existed, others were only thought to exist; some were created by story-tellers and others were a mixture of fact and fantasy. A few examples of monsters are shown on this page.

▲ Fifty thousand years ago, people in Europe hunted (or were hunted by) this terrifying, real-life monster. It is a *Smilodon*, a Saber-tooth Tiger. Its dagger-like teeth, used for stabbing its prey, grew up to 6 inches long.

▲ Before people understood the real causes for natural disasters, such as earthquakes, they often believed that monsters caused them. In the Middle East, an evil, smoke-like monster called a Jinn, shown above, was blamed for creating sandstorms.

Hen's egg

Aepyornis's egg

▲ People tried to please and soothe the monsters in various ways. Hai Ho Shang, a terrible Chinese sea monster, could be calmed by a sailor performing a dance to the beat of a gong It could also be frightened away by the smell of burning feathers which it hated.

▲ Today, most of the world has been mapped and photographed, but there are still a few unknown regions, such as the ocean depths. While they remain unexplored, there is still a chance that monsters, like the one above, may lurk somewhere.

▲ Many of the monsters of myth and legend have a factual basis. The giant bird called the Roc in the story of Sinbad the Sailor was probably based on the discovery of the giant eggs of this flightless bird. It is an *Aepyornis*, a giant ostrich that lived on the island of Madagascar, off the coast of Africa, until it became extinct in the 1660's. The bird must have been known to Arab traders and to sailors, who used to store rum in the bird's empty egg-shells.

Ancient Greece

The Ancient Greeks believed that the world was controlled by gods, goddesses and other supernatural creatures. Some of these creatures were monsters, half-human and half-beast or strange combinations of different animals.

The Greeks told tales about these gods and monsters and their encounters with humans. Often human heroes had to battle or outwit the monsters.

One of the most famous stories is *The Odyssey*, a long poem composed by Homer, which tells of the adventures of the Greek warrior Odysseus, as he sailed home from the battle of Troy.

▲ The Greeks were excellent sailors who explored and colonized the land around the Mediterranean Sea. The red area on the map shows the lands that they knew. Beyond these, lay unexplored regions where they thought that monsters might live.

▲ The Sirens were beautiful women with birds' wings and claws, who lured sailors to their island home with their hypnotic songs. When the sailors were shipwrecked on the rocks, the Sirens tore their victims to shreds and then devoured them.

One-eyed giants

Odysseus and his crew met many monsters on their journey. Once, they came to the island of the Cyclops—huge, one-eyed giants, who lived as shepherds. Odysseus and his men went ashore and took refuge in a cave which turned out to be the home of Polyphemus, the fiercest Cyclops of all. Polyphemus came back to the cave with his sheep. He blocked the entrance with a huge boulder.

Trapped inside the giant's lair, Odysseus had no choice but to approach Polyphemus and ask for his mercy. Instead of welcoming them, the giant seized two of the men and ate them. The next morning, he devoured two more and left the survivors shut inside the cave.

The Cyclops is blinded

Odysseus set to work on a plan of escape. He found a stake and sharpened its tip. That night, when the giant slept, Odysseus held the stake in the fire until it was red-hot, and then drove it into Polyphemus's only eye, blinding him. The giant roared with anger and pain, but could not see the men to kill them.

In the morning, Polyphemus rolled away the stone to let his flock out. To make sure that the men were not sneaking past, the giant felt the back of each sheep as it went by. But Odysseus tricked him once again. He and his men clung to the sheeps' bellies as they trotted out of the cave. In this way, they managed to escape from the Cyclops undetected.

Minotaur and Medusa

Among the most gruesome monsters of Greek legend are the Minotaur and the Gorgons. The Minotaur was a man with the head of a ferocious bull. The Gorgons were three sisters with snakes growing from their heads instead of hair. Any human who dared look them in the face was instantly turned to stone. Medusa was the most well known of the Gorgons.

Monster of the Labyrinth

The wife of King Minos of Crete gave birth to a horrible monster called the Minotaur. It was part bull, part man, and was imprisoned in a maze called the Labyrinth. The maze was so cleverly made that no one could find their way out of it.

The Minotaur ate only human flesh so King Minos had to provide living victims to be fed to the monster. Among the victims were fourteen young people that Athens had to pay in tribute to Crete yearly because the Athenians had been defeated in battle. Theseus, the son of the King of Athens, volunteered to go as one of the victims and to put an end to this cruel sacrifice by killing the monster.

The end of the Minotaur

When Theseus arrived in Crete, Ariadne, the daughter of Minos, fell in love with him. She gave him a ball of thread to help him with his task.

When Theseus entered the Labyrinth, he carefully tied one end of the thread to the entrance, and unwound the ball behind him as he went into the maze. When Theseus finally reached the hungry monster, he fought with it and managed to kill it. Then, by rewinding the thread, he was able to find his way out of the Labyrinth and rejoin Ariadne.

Medusa of the Gorgons

Medusa was once a beautiful woman, but the goddess Athena hated her and changed her into a monster. She became so hideous that anyone who looked at her was turned to stone.

A Greek hero called Perseus was set the impossible task of bringing back Medusa's head to win his bride. To help him, Athena gave Perseus a helmet which made him invisible, and a shining shield.

Armed with these, Perseus approached Medusa while she slept. Taking care not to look at her face, but only her reflection in the shield, he cut off Medusa's head and avoided being turned to stone.

Grendel

The Old English poem *Beowulf* is another story of a monster-slaying hero. This epic poem was written about 750 AD in northern England, but the poet remains unknown.

The poem tells the story of the hero Beowulf and his three battles with monsters. In his youth, Beowulf gains fame by killing the monster Grendel, who has been terrorizing the hall of King Hrothgar. Then he kills Grendel's mother, an even fiercer monster, when she tries to avenge her son.

In old age, Beowulf single-handedly fights and kills a dragon that is destroying his people, but he dies as a result of his wounds.

▲ Although Beowulf is thought to be a fictional character, there is some historical basis for the poem. King Hrothgar was a real fifth century Danish King, whose stronghold was located on the island of Zealand, off the mainland of Denmark.

The Dragon that killed Beowulf?

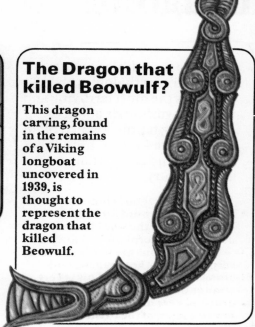

This dragon carving, found in the remains of a Viking longboat uncovered in 1939, is thought to represent the dragon that killed Beowulf.

The monster who hated music and dancing

Grendel was, in the words of the poem, a "mighty, monstrous fiend", who lived in the marshes near the stronghold of a Danish king called Hrothgar.

The King built a new banqueting hall for feasting. Every night, in his lair in the marshes, Grendel could hear the sounds of music and dancing coming from the hall. More than anything, the monster hated the sound of happiness and rejoicing.

Grendel's savage attack

One night, after the singing had stopped, Grendel stole across the marshes and crept into the great hall. He found Hrothgar's men lying asleep on the floor. He snatched thirty men and returned to his lair to devour them. Greedy for more human flesh, he raided the hall the next night and every night after that, until few of Hrothgar's men remained alive, and the hall stood empty.

Beowulf fights the monster

Beowulf, leader of a people called the Geats, was a great warrior, and when he heard of Grendel, he wanted to test his strength against the monster. He came to King Hrothgar and boasted that he could kill Grendel. A feast was held in the hall to attract the monster. When Grendel arrived, Beowulf wrestled with him for hours, until he managed to tear out one of Grendel's arms. The monster crept back to his lair to die.

Beowulf

Dragons!

Of all the incredible monsters of the world's mythologies, the dragon is the most terrifying and well-known. Stories about this giant flying reptile – which often breathes fire – are thousands of years old and come from nearly every country.

The name "dragon" comes from the ancient Greek word for serpent. In medieval tales the word "worm" was used for both serpents and dragons.

Some dragons are really just large serpents, but other dragons look almost like dinosaurs. This is very strange because the legends about dragons were invented long before any one knew of the existence of dinosaurs.

Dragons East and West

Although there are dragons in both Eastern and Western myths, they are quite different in appearance and behavior. In Chinese mythology, dragons are usually friendly and bring good fortune. Although they are often wingless, they can fly.

Western dragons are dark, ugly, fire-breathing serpents with wings. They have always been thought of as evil and so many stories tell of heroes who try to destroy them. St George is probably the most famous dragon-slayer. According to the legend, he came to a place which was terrorized by a dragon that demanded to be fed young maidens. St George fought and killed the dragon and rescued the beautiful maiden.

Some dragons had as many as seven heads.

Dragons of Western legends usually live in caves or underwater. They often guard a vast hoard of treasure.

Dragons can have either two or four legs with the claws of an eagle.

The heraldic dragon on shields and coats-of-arms has: a wolf's head, a serpent's body, a bat's wings, an eagle's talons and a barbed tongue and tail. It is officially known as "dragonée".

The dragon story

▲ Britain has many legends about dragons. One story tells of a ferocious battle between a red and a white dragon. They were finally captured when asleep and were buried in the Welsh mountains. The red dragon became a symbol of war, and it can still be seen on the Welsh flag.

▲ In Norse myths, dragons guarded the burial mounds of warriors. Because the dragon was a symbol of war, Vikings painted dragons on their shields and carved dragons' heads on the prows of their warships. This dragon carving was found in a Viking burial site in Norway.

▲ In Chinese mythology, dragons were rarely evil. They were the companions of the gods and cruised through the heavens, gathering clouds and rain. Dragons were believed to control the weather and especially the rains which helped crops to grow. People tried to

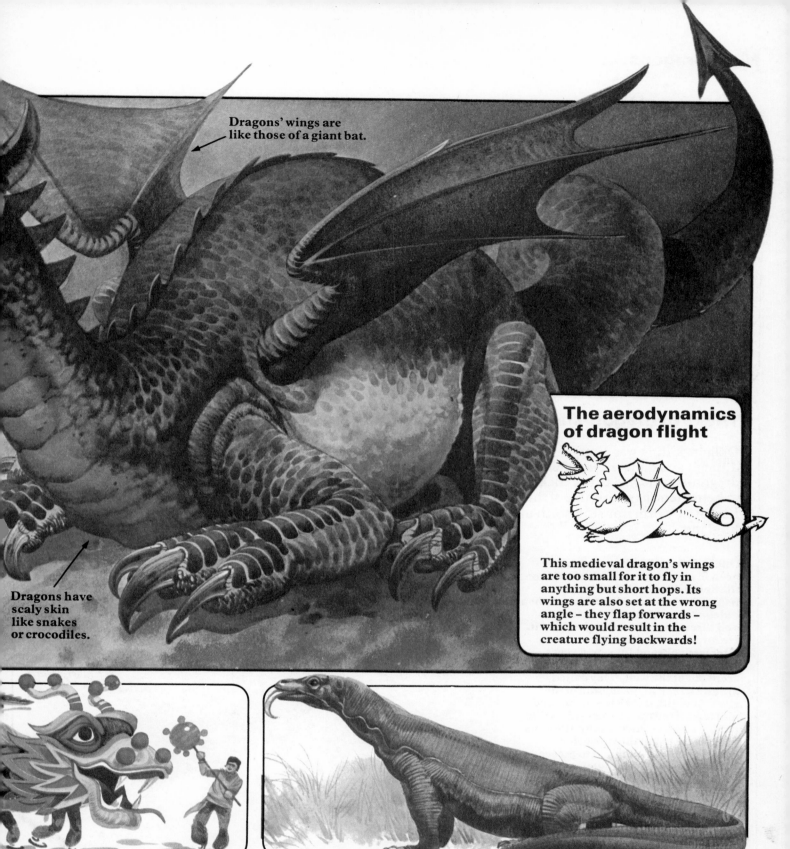

Dragons' wings are like those of a giant bat.

Dragons have scaly skin like snakes or crocodiles.

The aerodynamics of dragon flight

This medieval dragon's wings are too small for it to fly in anything but short hops. Its wings are also set at the wrong angle – they flap forwards – which would result in the creature flying backwards!

please the dragons so that there would be a good harvest. If the dragons were angered, they could cause a flood, a drought or an eclipse. Even today, people fly dragon kites and carry paper dragons (shown above) in the New Year's parade to bring good luck.

▲ In 1912 a report was published which announced the discovery of a kind of "dragon" living on the island of Komodo in Indonesia. For years, pearl fishermen, the only people visiting the uninhabited island, had told stories of a giant land crocodile on Komodo that ate pigs and goats. The reports were so insistent that finally a zoological expedition was sent to investigate. The "dragons" turned out to be an unknown species of Giant Monitor Lizard, which grows up to ten feet tall. The Komodo Dragon is the biggest lizard on earth.

More dragons....

The Shaggy Beast's deadly arsenal

Dragons caused vast destruction by spitting flames and using their deadly teeth and claws.
The monster in this story was equipped with an amazing range of other weapons as well.

In the Middle Ages a furry dragon, called the Shaggy Beast, terrorized a small, peaceful village in France. It raided farms, devoured children and young girls and ruined crops. Finally, a young man, seeking revenge for his dead sweetheart, cut the dragon's tail in two. This was the only place where it could be wounded and so it died.

Deadly stingers could be fired from its fur to maim and kill the creature's enemies.

Searing flames that destroyed crops

Tricks of dragon-slaying

Dragon-killing was always difficult and dangerous. Often the dragon-slayers had to use tricks to help them, as in this tale of the Lambton Worm from the north of England.

One Sunday, when he should have been in church, young John Lambton, the heir to Lambton Castle, was fishing in the River Wear. He caught a hideous worm, hauled it onto land and threw it into a well to get rid of it. He forgot about the worm and soon after went abroad for seven years.

But the worm grew enormous and crept out of the well. It lay coiled around a rock in the middle of the river. At night, it crawled up on land and terrorized the countryside, killing people and livestock. Many attempts were made to kill the worm, but whenever it was chopped to pieces, the pieces grew back together again!

When Lambton returned and learned what had happened, he was determined to destroy the monster. He went to consult a witch, who told him to stud his armor with razor-sharp spikes and to fight the monster in mid-stream.

The worm appeared and Lambton attacked it with his sword. When the monster coiled itself around him, the razor-studded armor cut it to shreds. The pieces of the worm fell into the river and were swept away before they could join up again.

Discovering dinosaurs

Until the 19th century, no one had the slightest idea that dinosaurs once lived on Earth. The first remains of such an animal were unearthed in a quarry in Oxfordshire, England, in 1822. The creature to which the remains belonged was named *Megalosaurus*, which means "big lizard". (The word "dinosaur" means "terrible lizard".)

Since then, over 800 fossils of the long-extinct dinosaurs have been discovered and studied. We now know that although some of the dinosaurs were fierce hunters, there were many others which were harmless plant-eaters.

Iguanodon is unearthed

In 1822, the remains of a plant-eating dinosaur were found in England by Dr and Mrs Gideon Mantell. The Mantells were travelling in Sussex, and made a stop near Cuckfield so that Dr Mantell could attend to a patient. Mrs Mantell wandered into the trees nearby, and noticed some teeth sticking out of the ground. She took them to show to her husband.

Although he was a keen fossil collector, he had never seen anything like them before. He sent them to an expert in Paris to find out which animal they came from.

Iguanodon gets its name

The expert identified them as being the upper front teeth of a rhinoceros. Dr Mantell refused to believe this, and took the fossils to the Museum in the Royal College of Surgeons, in London. There, they were compared with the teeth of a South American iguana, a type of lizard. They were much larger than the iguana's teeth, but the similarity was unmistakable. Dr Mantell decided, therefore, to call his discovery *"Iguanodon"*, which means "iguana tooth".

Reconstructing the monster

Dr Mantell spent five years searching for more evidence of *Iguanodon*. Eventually he found part of a skeleton, and from it a life-size model was built and displayed. It was not until 1878 that the model was found to be completely wrong.

In that year, some Belgian coal miners found a pit into which 31 *Iguanodon* had fallen to their deaths millions of years before. Their skeletons helped scientists to reconstruct a more accurate model of *Iguanodon*.

▲ In 1851, life-size models of dinosaurs were exhibited in London. They were based on fossils, and *Iguanodon* (above) was based on Dr Mantell's evidence. It was mistakenly shown walking on four legs. The horn placed on its snout was really a thumb-bone.

▼ Before the exhibition, a dinner was held inside the model's stomach. Twenty-one scientists and other guests drank a toast to *Iguanodon's* restoration. On page 13, you can see what this reptile really looked like and how it would have stood.

Lords of the world

For 140 million years, dinosaurs were the most important reptiles on Earth. More than 800 different kinds of dinosaurs developed during this period and they lived all over the world.

All the information we have about dinosaurs comes from studying their fossils. Some of these are bones and teeth that have, over the ages, turned into stone. Others include footprints, which tell us how dinosaurs stood and moved, patterns made on rocks by their skin, and fossils of dinosaur eggs. Scientists have even found the fossilized contents of dinosaurs' stomachs!

How the dinosaurs developed

The first true dinosaurs were flesh-eating reptiles. One of the earliest was *Ornithosuchus* (see chart below). It had clawed feet and powerful jaws to kill its prey. Scientists think that all the large flesh-eating dinosaurs which appeared later, developed from *Ornithosuchus*.

The smaller flesh-eating dinosaurs probably developed from the long-necked, slender *Coelophysis*. It could move its head quickly to snap up small animals, such as insects.

Plant-eating dinosaurs

Plant-eating dinosaurs developed later. Some species, like *Apatosaurus* (see chart below), grew to an enormous size. They became too heavy to walk upright, and moved along slowly on all fours. The biggest of all was *Brachiosaurus*, weighing 110 tons and standing over 38 feet tall–more than twice the height of a giraffe.

Dinosaurs with armor

Later, some of the plant-eating dinosaurs grew rows of bony plates on their backs to protect them from the flesh-eaters. The largest was *Stegosaurus* (see chart below), which weighed nearly 2.2 tons.

Another group grew flat bones on their bodies that covered them rather like a tortoise's shell. *Scolosaurus* (see right) was one of these.

Duck-billed and horned dinosaurs

There were hundreds of varieties of hadrosaurs, or duck-billed dinosaurs, such as *Anatosaurus* (see next page). They had flat, duck-like mouths containing rows of tightly-packed teeth. Some grew horny crests on their heads.

The horned dinosaurs, like *Triceratops*, were the last group to appear and develop.

The end of the dinosaurs

No one knows why the dinosaurs died out. Some people think that the plant-eating dinosaurs could not adapt to the new vegetation that was developing at that time. When they died, the flesh-eaters had no prey left.

Other people believe that the dinosaurs died out because of a change in the Earth's climate, bringing cold winters. Before this, the Earth had been warm all year. But now the dinosaurs lost all their body heat in the winter, and could not warm up again when the summers came. Many other theories have been put forward, but the puzzle is still unsolved.

Triceratops had three sharp horns, each up to 3 feet long, which it used to defend itself against flesh-eating dinosaurs. The entire animal was 36 feet long and weighed 9.4 tons.

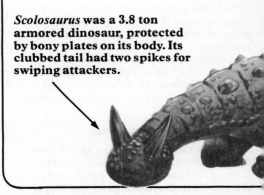

Scolosaurus was a 3.8 ton armored dinosaur, protected by bony plates on its body. Its clubbed tail had two spikes for swiping attackers.

The story of life

	PRE-CAMBRIAN 570	CAMBRIAN 500	ORDO-VICIAN 430	SILURIAN 395	DEVONIAN 345

This chart shows when the various kinds of animal life first appeared, beginning with the simple bacteria which existed in Pre-Cambrian times 570 million years ago.

The approximate dates of the pre-historic periods (given in millions of years before the present day) are shown beneath their geological names.

Dinosaurs lived in the Triassic, Jurassic and Cretaceous periods. After they died out, the Age of Mammals, or Tertiary period, began. Man did not appear until near the end of the Tertiary period.

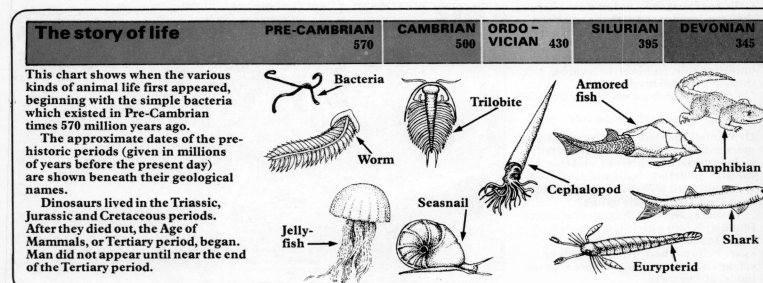

Bacteria

Trilobite

Armored fish

Worm

Cephalopod

Amphibian

Seasnail

Jelly-fish

Eurypterid

Shark

NOTE–The creatures shown on these two pages are not drawn to the same scale.

The long-tailed *Rhamphorhynchus* lived in the Jurassic period. It had long, sharp teeth for catching fish.

Spinosaurus lived in a very hot region. It had a "sail" of skin, held up by spines which grew from its backbone. This increased the surface area of its body, and probably helped it to cool down more quickly if it overheated.

Spiky thumb, at first thought to be a horn on *Iguanodon's* snout.

Pterosaurs were flying reptiles. They had leathery wings and furry bodies, like huge bats. Like the dinosaurs, they died out towards the end of the Cretaceous period.

This is the modern view of what *Iguanodon* looked like. Unlike the 19th-century model, it is now known to have walked on its hind legs.

ARBONIFEROUS	PERMIAN	TRIASSIC	JURASSIC	CRETACEOUS	TERTIARY 2½
280	225	190	136	65	Present day ⟶

Man

Dragonfly and other insects

Dimetrodon

Pterosaur

Apatosaurus

Triceratops

Mastodon

Hylonomus (a reptile)

Ornithosuchus

Stegosaurus

Duck-billed dinosaur

Lemur

Saber-tooth tiger

Ichthyosaur

Tyrannosaurus

13

The fiercest beast to walk the Earth?

Tyrannosaurus rex is the largest flesh-eating dinosaur yet discovered. It roamed the Earth 70 million years ago, in the Cretaceous period of prehistory. Its name means "king of the tyrant reptiles", and this huge beast must have had few enemies.

Standing erect on its massive back legs, it was 19½ feet tall, about 49 feet long and weighed more than 8 tons. Its greatest handicap was its tiny brain.

In spite of its powerful legs, *Tyrannosaurus* was too heavy to run fast, and the smaller, lighter dinosaurs could easily outpace it. Its clawed feet were used for killing and tearing its prey. Its front arms were so short that it probably only used them for picking its teeth, and for pushing itself off the ground after resting.

Its razor-sharp teeth were 6 inches long and could have sliced up the flesh of dead dinosaurs quite easily. One large meal would probably have lasted *Tyrannosaurus* several weeks, so it may have spent a lot of time resting and sleeping.

Gigantic killer

Tyrannosaurus rex, **shown here to scale with a man, had a stiff tail which swept from side to side as the animal waddled along. The heavy tail helped** *Tyrannosaurus* **to balance itself, as the top half of its body was so massive.**

The landscape of the late Cretaceous period looked similar to that of today's woodlands.

Tyrannosaurus **was armed with thick, curved talons as well as blade-like teeth. The animal it is attacking is a duck-billed dinosaur.**

An agile *Ornithomimus* **running off with a piece of flesh.**

Tyrannosaurus ate whatever it could catch. Slow-moving, plant-eating dinosaurs, like the duck-billed *Anatosaurus* on the left, were a typical prey. They lived in large groups as a defense against the flesh-eaters. Group defense is used by lots of creatures. Staying in a group, an animal is less likely to be caught by a predator than if it lives by itself.

Serpents in the sea

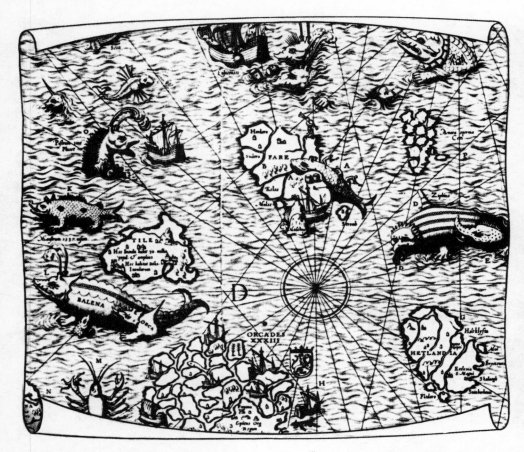

Oceans cover more than two-thirds of the Earth's surface, and in places reach a depth of 6½ miles. This underwater world has not yet been thoroughly explored, so it is possible that unknown monsters exist there.

Between the 17th century and the present day, there have been hundreds of detailed sightings of terrifying creatures at sea. These are most often described as giant squid and octopuses (see pages 18-19) or as "sea serpents".

Reports of sea serpents say they look like smooth snakes, but they are many times larger than the biggest snakes on Earth: the longest seem to be about 650 feet.

They are said to be yellow or mottled brown in color, often with seaweed-like manes. Their heads can be up to ten feet long, equipped with curving teeth. They seem to have neither fins nor limbs, and they twist and turn through the water like snakes.

▲ In the 16th century, when this map was made, little was known about creatures that lived in remote areas of the globe. Map-makers decorated their maps with imaginary beasts.

▶ The serpent found by *Monongahela's* crew may have looked like this. Mariners' tales, often exaggerated by retelling, are the main source of information about sea monsters.

Monongahela's monster

In 1852, two whaling ships, the *Monongahela* and the *Rebecca Sims*, from New Bedford (see map on right), were sailing alongside each other in the Pacific. A look-out reported a whale off the port bow. The master of the *Monongahela*, Captain Seabury, launched three longboats to go after it.

As they drew near their prey, the sailors realized that they were dealing with something much more fierce than any whale. Seabury nevertheless decided to tackle it, and thrust a harpoon deep into the creature's neck. It died within minutes, but not before sinking the other two longboats with its thrashings.

The sailors hauled in their amazing catch. The captain of the *Rebecca Sims* described it in the ship's log as a brownish-gray reptile at least 150 feet long. In its great jaws were dozens of sharp and curving teeth.

The body was too large to bring on board, so the head was cut off and preserved in a pickling vat aboard the *Monongahela*.

The monster is lost

The two ships then started back for their home port. The *Rebecca Sims* returned safely, but the other ship was never seen again. No trace of its crew, nor of the monster's head, was ever found. Only some wreckage was washed up, off the coast of Alaska.

The North Sea Terror

In 1881, a Scottish fishing boat, the *Bertie,* was 87 miles out in the North Sea. Suddenly, the crew noticed three humps breaking the surface of the water, and then part of a head draped with a growth that looked like seaweed. Two fierce eyes glared at the terror-stricken sailors.

The creature headed straight for the boat. The crew tried to drive it away, and one man fired a rifle at it. The "serpent" churned the water, almost capsizing the boat.

Fishing gear was thrown off the deck and two of the crew were pitched violently backwards into the hold.

The fishermen cut their lines and set sail for port, but the sea serpent continued to follow them. When night fell, the crew lost sight of the strange monster.

Panic in the fog

In 1962, off the Florida coast, an American Air Force raft, carrying five skin-divers, was swept out to sea in a storm. As the storm cleared, dense fog came down.

After they had been stranded for about an hour, they heard splashing and noticed a smell of dead fish, then a hissing noise. Suddenly, what looked like a brown, slimy neck, about 13 feet long, reared up out of the water. The creature's head was shaped like a sea turtle's. One diver saw the neck bend and the head dip into the water several times. The divers panicked and leapt into the sea. In the fog, they lost sight of one another. According to the only survivor, his comrades went under one by one, screaming in terror. They were never found.

Monongahela's route

NORTH AMERICA

New Bedford

Serpent sighted here

Whaling grounds

SOUTH AMERICA

Route of the *Monongahela*

The riddle of the Kraken

"Kraken" is an old Norse word used to describe giant sea creatures that mariners reported they had seen. They were said to be shaped like squid or octopuses, with many arms that could pluck men from ships, and even drag whole boats to the bottom of the sea.

Although many of the stories are exaggerated accounts, and were once thought to be only legends, there is now proof that giant squid do exist. Parts of squid and even whole bodies of enormous size have been found. They have been examined by experts in many different parts of the world.

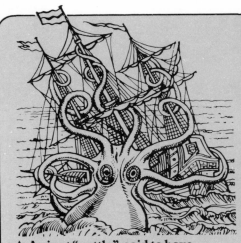

▲ A giant "cuttle", said to have wrapped its tentacles round the masts of an 18th-century slave ship.

Fight with a kraken

In 1873, two men and a boy were fishing in a rowing boat off the coast of Newfoundland, when one of the men stuck a boathook into a mass of floating wreckage. Suddenly, the "wreckage" jerked to life. It was an enormous sea monster. Two of its tentacles shot out to grasp the little boat.

The creature began to sink beneath the water, pulling the boat along with it. As the sea flooded around them, the boy grabbed an axe and hacked at the slithery tentacles. As he cut at them, the monster released a jet of black ink, withdrew and disappeared.

The fishermen reached the shore unharmed and took a piece of tentacle to show to a local naturalist called Moses

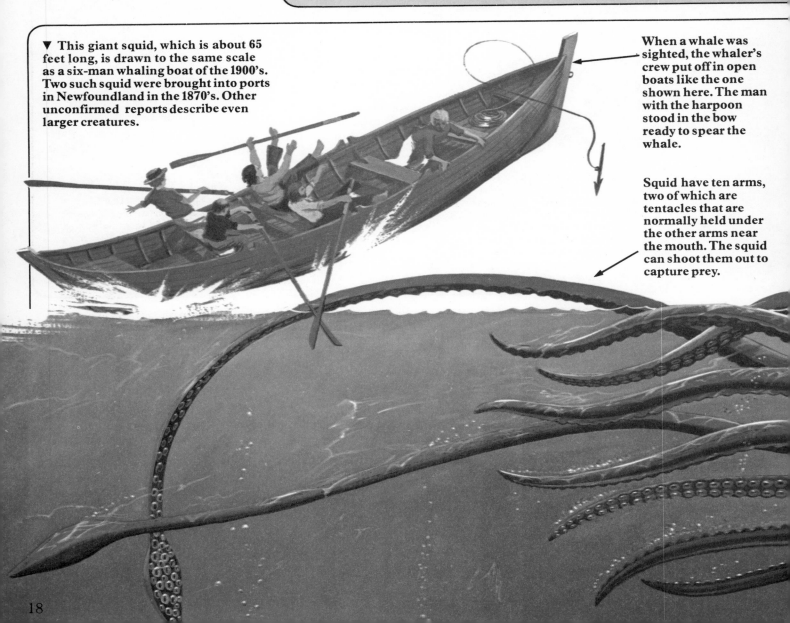

▼ This giant squid, which is about 65 feet long, is drawn to the same scale as a six-man whaling boat of the 1900's. Two such squid were brought into ports in Newfoundland in the 1870's. Other unconfirmed reports describe even larger creatures.

When a whale was sighted, the whaler's crew put off in open boats like the one shown here. The man with the harpoon stood in the bow ready to spear the whale.

Squid have ten arms, two of which are tentacles that are normally held under the other arms near the mouth. The squid can shoot them out to capture prey.

Harvey. He was amazed by the specimen, which was very tough and 20 feet long.

More proof is found

A month later, four other men brought Harvey a similar creature. They said they had been bringing in one of their nets, which had seemed very heavy. When they got it to the surface, they had seen a writhing mass of jelly, from which two fierce eyes had peered at them. They had battled with it until one of them killed it.

Moses Harvey bought the creature from the fishermen for ten dollars. He took several photographs of it and sent them off to London. There, scientists who examined it declared that it was a giant squid—one of the largest ever found.

In 1887, another giant squid was found, this time in New Zealand. Its body measured about ten feet, and its tentacles were another 43 feet long. As recently as 1964, a 36-foot squid was found in the sea near La Corunna, in Spain.

Monsters of the deep

Even today, we do not know exactly how large squid can grow. One estimate is based on the size of marks found on the heads of some sperm whales (who eat mainly squid). These are scars left by the squids' suckers on the whales' skin. The whales seem to have fought with squid at least 80 feet long.

▲ A sea monster described in a book in the 16th century.

A squid is an invertebrate (an animal without a backbone), that is related to the octopus and the cuttlefish. Squid have circular suckers on each of their arms. As well as giant squid like this one, there are small ones, about 8 inches long.

The squid can contract its body suddenly, forcing out a strong jet of water, which propels it backwards. It can also squirt out ink to confuse its enemies.

Giant squid live in deep open water, but may come to the surface of the sea in search of food. Their diet includes shellfish and fish. They are pursued and eaten by toothed whales. Bodies of giant squid have been found in sperm whales' stomachs.

▲ Some people think that the idea of sea serpents arose from sightings of giant squid. If a squid was under the water, and raised one tentacle above the surface, as in this picture, this could appear to be a snake-like head and neck.

The Abominable Snowman...

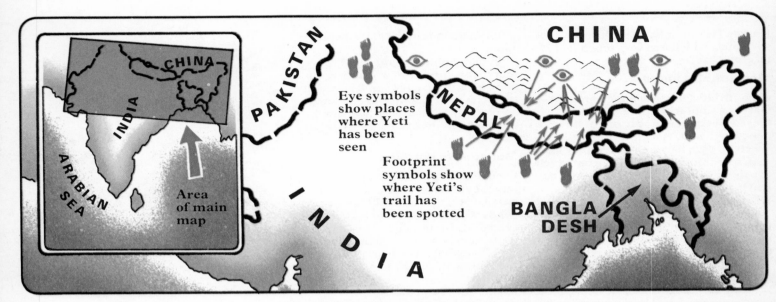

▲ This map shows the places where people claim to have seen Yetis or their tracks. Unidentified ape-like creatures have also been seen in other places, such as high in the Pamir mountains, north of Pakistan.

Over the last 100 years, reports have come in from many parts of the world of a man-like beast that walks upright and is covered in shaggy hair. These unknown animals have many names, but in the countries spanned by the Himalayan mountains, it is called the Yeti, or Abominable Snowman.

The reports differ, but many of them agree on the following features: the creature is about 6½ feet tall when standing upright, and has a powerful body completely covered in reddish-brown hair. It has long arms that reach to its knees and a hairless face that looks like an ape's. It is said to be shy and not aggressive to humans.

It has been seen both in the forested areas on the lower slopes of the Himalayas and higher up, in the snowfields. It seems to be active mainly at night and is usually alone, although it has been seen in pairs. Some observers say that it eats goats and other mammals, while others say it is a vegetarian. No one has ever managed to capture or to photograph a Yeti.

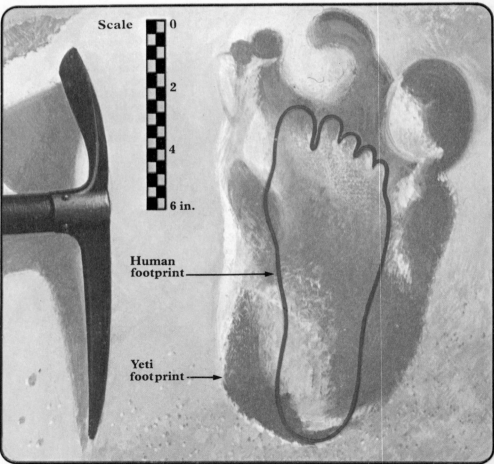

▲ In 1951, a British explorer, Eric Shipton, found a long set of Yeti footprints on the Menlung Glacier, near the border between Nepal and Tibet (now part of China). He took a photograph of them alongside an ice-pick handle. The prints were 13 in. long and 8 in. wide.

They clearly showed an unusually long, thick second toe. The tracks showed where the animal had jumped a crevasse, digging its toes deeply into the ice to prevent itself from falling. Whatever made the tracks looked as though it walked on two feet.

Encounters in the snow

In 1942, seven Polish prisoners escaped from a Soviet labor camp in Siberia. In his book which describes their journey, Slavomir Rawicz tells how they encountered two Yetis.

As the men crossed the Himalayas on their way to India, they saw two creatures on a rocky shelf about 100 yards away from them. Rawicz says they were nearly 8 feet tall and covered in long hair. They resembled apes or bears and shuffled about on the ledge for two hours while the men watched them. They showed no signs of fear, even though they were aware of the onlookers.

Although his report is one of the most detailed ever recorded, some people doubt that it is all true.

Yeti or spy?

During the Second World War, in 1941, a Soviet army doctor in the Caucasus was asked to examine a man thought to be a spy. The man had been found in the mountains.

"He was obviously a man", said the doctor, "because his entire shape was human. Yet he had shaggy hair ¾ or one inch long all over his body. He stood before me like a proud giant but his eyes were dull and empty like the eyes of an animal. He was not a spy in disguise, but some kind of wild man".

A cliff-top sighting

A Russian scientist, Dr Pronin, of Leningrad University, claims to have glimpsed the Yeti in 1958. Dr Pronin was studying glaciers in the Pamirs when he saw a figure outlined on top of a cliff about 440 yards away from him. He described the creatures as thick-set, long-armed and covered in reddish-gray hair.

"It walked out of a cave for about 220 yards or so, and then vanished over the edge of the cliff", reported Dr Pronin. He said that the creature was known to the local villagers as "the wild man".

...and its cousin, the Sasquatch

The Sasquatch is a man-like beast similar to the Yeti, and is said to live in the remote forests of North America. This name, which means "hairy giant", was given to it by the North American Indians, but it is also known as Bigfoot.

Since the first report of this creature by a white man in 1811, there have been hundreds of sightings. Bigfoot is usually described as being over 6½ feet tall, and footprints 16 inches long have been found. As yet, however, no one has managed to prove Bigfoot's existence.

Among other things, Bigfoot is supposed to have interrupted picnics, grappled with moving cars, and actually walked into people's homes. A lumberjack named Albert Ostman claimed that in 1924 he was kidnapped by a whole family of "near human hairy beasts" in British Columbia but managed to escape.

The hungry Sasquatch

The Sasquatch is said to live on roots, berries and leaves in the summer, and on any sort of meat (from rats to cows) in the winter. This diet is similar to that of the bears that live in North America. The creature is also reported to have stolen fish, doughnuts and, on one occasion, chocolate.

▲ This map shows that most Sasquatch sightings occur in the mountainous regions near the Pacific coast. The black dots show places where Sasquatch has been sighted or prints found.

▶ In 1967, Roger Patterson, a keen Bigfoot tracker, went to Bluff Creek Valley in California to look for signs of the monster. He claims to have come across a female Bigfoot, and to have taken a film of her. One frame from the film is shown here, with the Bigfoot arrowed. Professor John Napier, an expert on the human body and the mechanics of walking, studied the film and said that it was probably a hoax.

Confusing footprints

Many people have said that the Sasquatch footprints were not made by an unknown beast at all, but were those of various well-known animals, or of human beings. The feet of some of these animals are shown here, along with a human foot and a reconstruction of a Sasquatch foot, based on footprints found. The human foot looks most like the Sasquatch foot, in shape if not in size.

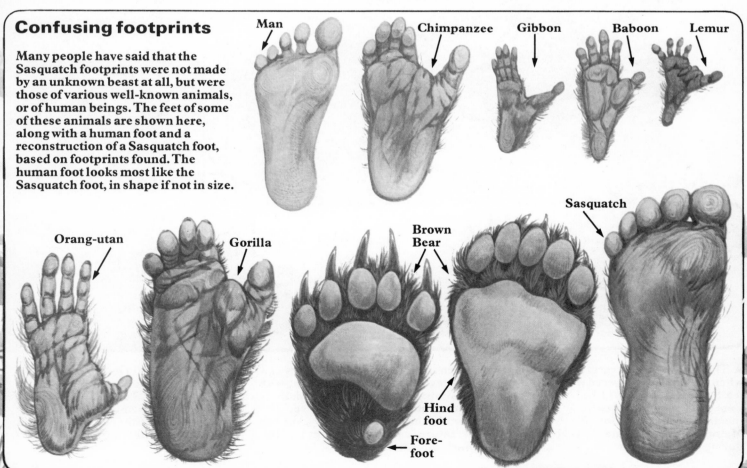

Man   Chimpanzee   Gibbon   Baboon   Lemur

Orang-utan   Gorilla   Brown Bear   Sasquatch   Hind foot   Fore-foot

Monsters in the loch

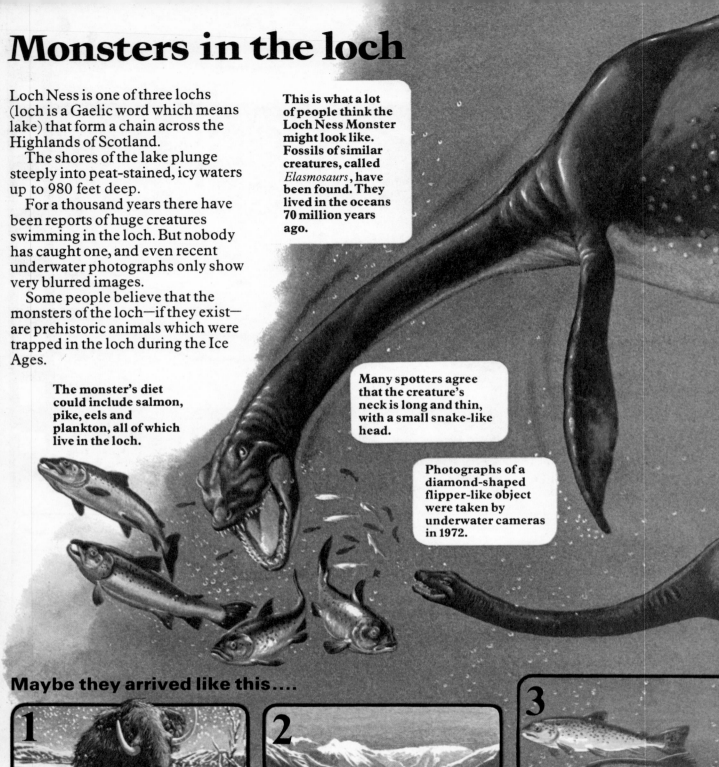

Loch Ness is one of three lochs (loch is a Gaelic word which means lake) that form a chain across the Highlands of Scotland.

The shores of the lake plunge steeply into peat-stained, icy waters up to 980 feet deep.

For a thousand years there have been reports of huge creatures swimming in the loch. But nobody has caught one, and even recent underwater photographs only show very blurred images.

Some people believe that the monsters of the loch—if they exist—are prehistoric animals which were trapped in the loch during the Ice Ages.

This is what a lot of people think the Loch Ness Monster might look like. Fossils of similar creatures, called *Elasmosaurs*, have been found. They lived in the oceans 70 million years ago.

The monster's diet could include salmon, pike, eels and plankton, all of which live in the loch.

Many spotters agree that the creature's neck is long and thin, with a small snake-like head.

Photographs of a diamond-shaped flipper-like object were taken by underwater cameras in 1972.

Maybe they arrived like this....

1

2

3

▲ There have been several Ice Ages, when the land was covered with thick ice. Steep-sided valleys like Loch Ness were gouged out of the earth by slow-moving mountains of ice. Wooly Mammoths like the one above lived during these Ice Ages.

▲ When the ice melted 12,000 years ago, the sea level rose. Loch Ness, along with other similar valleys, was flooded. It became a long, thin arm of the sea, rather like the fiords of Norway. Various sea creatures came to live in the newly-formed salt-water inlets.

▲ The land was no longer crushed by billions of tons of ice, so it gradually rose. Eventually Loch Ness was cut off from the North Sea. The sea creatures still in the loch either adapted to their new life in the lake, or they died out.

Some famous sightings

The earliest written reference to a monster in Loch Ness was in the diaries of St Columba, an English missionary in Scotland, in about AD 565. He writes of attending the burial of a man who had been bitten to death by a water beast while swimming.

An underwater shock

Much later, in 1880, a diver, Duncan McDonald, was sent to examine a sunken ship at the western end of the loch. Within minutes of reaching the wreck, he made frantic signals to be brought to the surface.

Witnesses said that he came out trembling violently. He claimed to have seen an enormous animal lying on a shelf of rock: "It was an odd-looking beastie", he said, "like a huge frog". He refused to dive in Loch Ness ever again.

The Mackays meet the monster

In 1933 the first motor road was built alongside the loch. In April of that year Mr and Mrs John MacKay were driving along the road when Mrs MacKay noticed a disturbance on the surface of the loch. At first she thought it was made by fighting ducks. Suddenly the splashing was replaced by a large V-shaped wake made by something moving at great speed.

When the wake was about 440 yards from shore, two large humps appeared. They moved in a line, with the rear one looking larger than the front one. The MacKays got out of their car and watched "an enormous animal rolling and plunging" until it disappeared with a huge splash.

The monster on land

Since 1933, 3,000 people claim to have seen the monster, and it is interesting that many of them describe a V-shaped wake, terrific disturbance of the water surface, and several humps being visible.

Other accounts speak of large unidentified animals on land around the lakeside. In 1934, Arthur Grant was travelling by motorcycle on the road by the loch, when he saw the monster. He says it crossed the road in front of him in two bounds and disappeared into the water. It had small, flipper-like forelimbs and was about 20 feet long.

Danger on the loch

In 1960, the Lowrie family were on the loch in their motor yacht, when they saw a form that looked like "two ducks... and a neck-like protrusion breaking surface". Mr Lowrie only had time to take four photographs, one of which showed a V-shaped wake, before changing course to avoid a collision with the creature.

A year earlier, the monster had been seen by a couple who were driving their car on the southern side of the loch. They said that a huge animal, with a long neck and a small head emerged from the bushes at the side of the road, carrying a dead lamb in its mouth. Then it plunged into the loch and disappeared.

▲ This map shows Loch Ness as it is today – a narrow lake 24 miles long, cut off from the sea. When the floor and sides of the lake were studied, with equipment normally used for detecting shipwrecks on the seabed, large underwater caves were found.

▲ This photograph was taken by a doctor, Colonel Robert Wilson, in 1934. He also took a picture of the head as it sank into the water. The ripples on the surface seem to indicate that there is a body under the water as well as the head and neck that are visible.

▲ The best-known landmark of Loch Ness is the ruin of Castle Urquahart. The castle is half-way along the northern shore and has proved to be the most popular spot from which to catch a glimpse of the monster.

Scientists investigate Loch Ness

▲ In 1938, a fish like the one above was caught off the coast of South Africa. It was a *Coelacanth,* and scientists thought that it had been extinct for 70 million years. Perhaps the Loch Ness Monster will also prove to be a survivor of the past, but as yet, no one has proof.

◄ This picture is based on a photograph taken in 1972 at the bottom of the loch by an American team. It shows a diamond-shaped flipper, apparently attached to the side of an animal. The flipper was reckoned to be about 6½ feet long.

► This submarine, the Vickers Oceanic *Pisces,* was used to try to track down the monster in Loch Ness in 1969. It had a sonar screen, but did not collect any definite evidence about the monster. Another submarine, the *Viperfish,* had no success either.

For the monster-hunters of Loch Ness, there are many problems. First, the loch is too large to be kept under constant watch. Thick mists often cover the surface, and under the water it is very hard to see anything clearly, because of particles of peat in the water.

People are constantly trying out new methods of recording evidence of large animals in the loch. The photographs taken by an American team in 1972 and 1975 caused a sensation when they were published. To many people, they were proof of the monster's existence. Other people were not so sure.

The first underwater photographs

In 1972, an American team at Loch Ness managed to take some underwater photographs. One picture appeared to be of an animal's flipper. Others showed what looked like a whole body.

The team used a camera which took a picture every time an electronic light flashed (about once every minute). It was linked to a sonar beam which bounced a pulse of high-pitched sound off objects and "blipped" their shape on to a screen in a boat above.

Even with such highly-developed equipment, the pictures were very murky and blurred. If the monster did exist, which many people still doubted, scientists disagreed over what kind of animal could be in the photographs.

Is the monster a prehistoric reptile?

The "flipper" above is unlike that of any known water creature. Some people suggest that it is rather like the limbs of some prehistoric reptiles. But the idea that "Nessie" is a relative of an early reptile has been rejected by some scientists.

They argue that the icy waters of a Scottish lake are no place for what was once a tropical marine reptile. They also say that if such an animal had survived, it would be more likely to have streamlined limbs, and not oar-shaped "flippers" as in the photo.

The argument about the monster's identity continued when the Americans produced a photo of a "head" in 1975. Some people argued that the horned "face" was more likely to be the prow of a sunken Viking ship, or even a piece of rotten wood.
It did not look like any animal that is known today, either living or extinct.

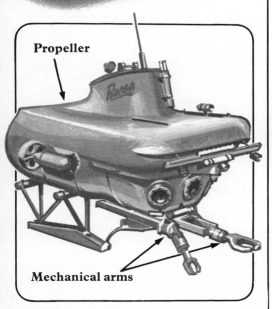

Propeller

Mechanical arms

Other lake monsters

Loch Ness is only one of about a dozen Scottish lakes that claims to have its own water monster. The number is just as high in Ireland. Similar animals have been reported swimming in freshwater lakes all over the world, and most of them before the Loch Ness monster was even heard of. A surprising number of these reports describe a creature with several humps and a small head on a long neck.

One Swedish monster, which is said to live in Lake Storsjö, was first heard of 80 years ago, when it chased two girls along the edge of the lake. The outraged locals made the cruel trap shown below for it. The creature appeared again, but fortunately was never caught in the trap.

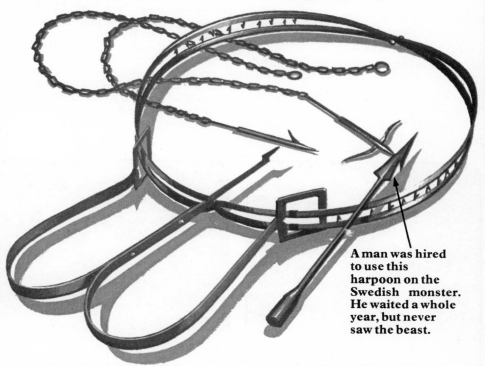

A man was hired to use this harpoon on the Swedish monster. He waited a whole year, but never saw the beast.

Those who doubt the monster's existence ask why no dead bodies have been washed ashore, and no bones have been found. If, as is claimed, the loch has been a breeding colony for 12,000 years, surely there would be better evidence of the monster's presence by now. One reply to this suggests that the monsters eat stones to help their digestion; when they die, their bodies sink to the bottom of the loch.

Another possible explanation of some of the sightings was discovered in Norway on a lake said to contain monsters. Twice, people saw what looked like humps on the surface of the water, and rowed out to see the "Hvaler Serpent", as the monster was known. They found that the "humps" were nothing more than large mats of rotting vegetation, buoyed up by marsh gas.

▼ The map below shows where some of the world's lake monsters are thought to live. They are usually associated with deep, remote lakes, surrounded by steep shores or mountains. Many of the monsters are said to churn up the surface of the water, and to look like upturned boats.

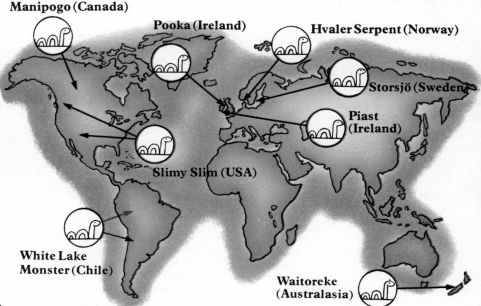

Manipogo (Canada)

Pooka (Ireland)

Hvaler Serpent (Norway)

Storsjö (Sweden)

Piast (Ireland)

Slimy Slim (USA)

White Lake Monster (Chile)

Waitoreke (Australasia)

Man-made monsters

Monsters have always been a popular subject for horror stories, and since the beginning of the century, they have also terrified and fascinated thousands of movie audiences.

The task of making movie monsters as frightening as possible is the job of the "special effects" department in the film studio.

The monsters are usually either models (life-size or miniature) or actors wearing special costumes and make-up. The models are mechanized, so that they can move about, or else trick photography is used to make them look as though they are moving.

The first *King Kong* film appeared in 1933. It tells the story of a giant ape that is captured on a remote island and brought to New York. There it escapes and climbs to the top of the Empire State Building, clutching the screaming heroine. The monster finally meets its end when it plummets to the ground. The scenes of the ape were shot using six small models (made of rubber and rabbit fur) and a giant one of its head and shoulders, covered in bear skin.

Mechni-Kong (shown above) was built for a Japanese film, in which this colossal robot fights with the giant ape, King Kong. It is equipped with a death ray, mounted in its head.

In *Frankenstein*, the nameless monster is played by a heavily-made-up actor. In the story, Baron Frankenstein brings the monster to life by passing an electric current through its body.

For the film *Jaws*, about a giant shark, three full-size mechanical models were made. They were each packed with electronic and other equipment to make the different parts of the shark move.

In the film *2001 A Space Odyssey*, the "monster" is a computer called HAL 9000. The computer, which forms part of a spaceship on a mission to Jupiter, kills all but one of the crew and has to be destroyed. The film makes spectacular use of special effects to give the impression of travelling through space. The ship, shown above, was a model 60 feet long. A model was also made to show the planet Jupiter.

Many films have been made about Godzilla, an enormous prehistoric reptile that is aroused by an atomic explosion. In *Godzilla*, it destroys Tokyo, crunching up the city's trains (shown above).

A full-scale model of a giant squid was built for the film *20,000 Leagues Under the Sea* (made in 1954). The mechanical model weighed several tons, and had to be worked by a team of 16 men. At one point in the film, the squid attacks a submarine, called the *Nautilus,* and threatens to crush the vessel, along with her crew, with its enormous tentacles. This battle was filmed in a giant-sized water tank in the film studios.

In *The Mummy,* made in 1932, a mummified ancient Egyptian suddenly comes to life, leaves his tomb, and searches for a long-lost love. He murders and terrorizes people who stand in his way.

Making a monster

1

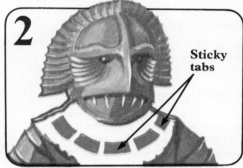

2

Sticky tabs

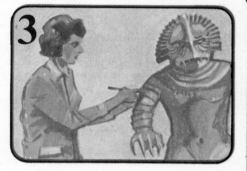

3

▲ These pictures show one way in which a "monster" can be made for films or television. First, the designer reads the script and sketches out his ideas. The monster in this case is a swamp creature, to be played by an actor in a special suit.

▲ The designer then discusses his ideas with the producer of the film. He decides to make the suit in separate pieces, stuck together with sticky tabs. This means that the costume can be used again if new parts, such as arms or a head, are added.

▲ The finished design is sent to a modeling unit. They first make a full-size clay model, scaled to fit the actor who will wear the suit. The clay model is then used to make a mold for the suit, which is cast in stretchy latex rubber.

4

5 The finished creature

▶ Before the film can be made, the actor has to learn to move inside the suit, and to cope with any special problems, such as overheating, which the costume may give him. On the film set, the monster can be made to seem even more menacing by means of different camera angles, lighting and sound effects.

▲ The rubber suit is then painted to make it look like rough skin. When the costume is finished, the actor tries it on for size. The zipper up the back is hidden by a flap which blends in with the scaly "skin."

A dictionary of monsters

This dictionary of monsters includes some of the creatures in this book as well as others which have not been mentioned. Some of these beasts are mythical, while others really did exist.

AMPHISBAENA Legendary Greek beast, with a second head growing from its tail, that could move backwards and forwards. When one head was asleep, the other stayed awake to keep watch.

ANUBIS Ancient Egyptian god of the dead which had the body of a man and the head of a jackal.

BASILISK In Greek myth a creature whose poisonous touch or glance meant certain death. Only three things could kill it: a weasel, a cock crowing or the sight of itself in a mirror.

BERBALANGS Malaysians believed in these ghouls that looked like humans except for their wings and slit eyes. They dug up graves to eat dead bodies.

CERBERUS In Greek myths a ferocious watchdog that guarded the gates of hell . It was usually imagined as having three heads.

CHIMERA From Greek mythology a fierce monster with a lion's head, a goat's body and a serpent's tail. Sometimes it had three heads. It breathed fire.

CYCLOPS In Greek legends a tribe of one-eyed giants. See page 5.

DRAGONS Giant flying reptiles in tales from all over the world. See pages 8-10.

FRANKENSTEIN'S MONSTER An artificial man, made of parts of dead human bodies, which came to life. See page 28.

GANESHA Elephant-headed god of wisdom in Indian mythology. He had a fat, red human body, four arms and one large tusk. He rode on the back of a rat.

GRENDEL Flesh-eating monster who fought with the hero Beowulf. See page 7.

GRIFFIN Ancient mythical beast from the Middle East, which was as strong as a hundred eagles. It had the head, wings and talons of an eagle with the hind legs and tail of a lion. It made a nest of gold which it guarded fiercely.

HAI HO SHANG Legendary monster fish with a shaven head which terrorized the South China Sea. It seized boats and drowned their crews.

HARPIES These creatures from Greek mythology had the head and breasts of a woman and the wings and claws of an eagle. They were foul-smelling, filthy beasts with monstrous appetites.

HYDRA Legendary Greek water serpent with many hideous human heads–stories vary from nine to one hundred heads. Each time a head was cut off, two new ones grew in its place.

KAPPA Legendary Japanese goblin with head of an ape, the body of a tortoise and a frog's legs. It lived in rivers, drowning and devouring people.

Griffin

KRAKEN Many-armed sea monster in Nordic legends. See pages 18-19.

KING KONG There are many popular horror films about this giant ape that rampaged through New York City. See page 28.

LAMBTON WORM Enormous dragon that terrorized an English village. See page 10.

LAMIAS These creatures of Greek myths were beautiful women from the waist upwards, but writhing serpents below the waist. With their beautiful whistling, they lured lost travellers to their den and ate them.

LOCH NESS MONSTER Large water creature reported to live in a Scottish Loch. See pages 24-27.

MAKARA Sea monster in Indian legends that was half-fish and half-mammal but the combinations varied.

MANTICORE This weird mythological creature had a man's head with blue eyes and three rows of teeth. It had a lion's body and a scorpion's tail covered with spines that it could shoot like arrows.

MEDUSA In Greek legends a winged monster with snakes on her head. See page 6.

MINOTAUR Monster that was half-man and half-bull in Greek myths. See page 6.

MOA Giant, ostrich-like bird, over 10 feet tall, that lived in New Zealand until the 18th century. It defended itself by kicking its strong legs.

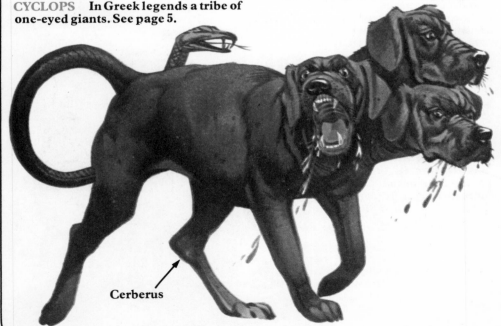

Cerberus

Scylla

NAGAS   These creatures of Indian mythology had snake-like bodies and human heads. They lived in palaces underground or in the water and had power over water–the seas, rivers and the rain.

NANDI BEAR   Giant, flesh-eating bear which the people of the Nandi tribe in East Africa believe roams about after dark. It utters blood-curdling shrieks. Its footprints are four times the size of a human's.

NASNAS   This horrific creature, in legends from the Middle East, is like a human being divided in half. It has half a face and body and only one arm and one leg.

OGRES   These man-eating giants are common in legends of many countries. They are always very ugly, and in Japanese stories their bodies are red and blue and they have teeth like elephants' tusks.

PTERODACTYL   Prehistoric flying reptiles that ate flesh. See page 13.

ROC   This immense eagle-like bird, with a wingspan of 90 feet, appears in the Arabian legend of "Sinbad the Sailor". It was said to be so huge that it could eat an elephant, grasping the animal with its huge talons.

Roc

SALAMANDER   Unlike the real lizard, this mythical reptile was said to live in fires. It had a deadly poisonous bite.

SASQUATCH   Shaggy-haired, ape-like man which has been reported in remote regions of North America. See pages 22-23.

SCYLLA   In Greek mythology this six-headed serpent lived in a cave on the coast of Sicily. It snatched and devoured passing sailors.

SEA SERPENTS   These large, unidentified monsters have been sighted in oceans all over the world. See pages 16-19.

SIMURG   Giant mythical bird that lived on the highest mountain in ancient Persia.

SPHINX   In Greek mythology this creature had a woman's head and breasts, a bird's wings and a lion's body and feet. She asked travellers riddles and if they could not answer, she devoured them.

SQUONK   American folktales tell of this timid beast that lives in the forests of Pennsylvania. It cries because of its wart-covered, ill-fitting skin. If captured, it dissolves itself in tears.

TENGU   Legendary Japanese monsters that were part human and part bird with huge claws and beaks. They had ferocious, glittering eyes.

THOTH   The ancient Egyptian moon god, who had the body of a man, and the head of an ibis.

TYRANNOSAURUS REX   This enormous prehistoric reptile was the largest, flesh-eating dinosaur that has yet been discovered. See pages 14-15.

WEREWOLVES   Folktales from all over the world tell of people who are transformed into wolves at every full moon, when they kill and devour humans. The only way to kill them is with a silver bullet.

WYVERN   Mythical flying serpent, much like a dragon but with an eagle's talons. Its sudden appearance was thought to herald the outbreak of war or plague.

YALE   Horse-like monster with a goat's beard, a boar's tusk and an elephant's tail. It could swivel its huge horns from back to front when it was fighting its enemies.

YETI   Huge, hairy man-like creature sometimes sighted in the Himalayas. See pages 20-21.

Werewolf

Index